BOB MARLEY
Piano Duet

Arranged by Brent Edstrom

ISBN 978-1-4803-9524-4

HAL•LEONARD®
CORPORATION

7777 W. BLUEMOUND RD. P.O. BOX 13819 MILWAUKEE, WI 53213

Visit Hal Leonard Online at
www.halleonard.com

BUFFALO SOLDIER

Buffalo Soldier, Dreadlock Rasta: there was a buffalo soldier in the heart of America,
Stolen from Africa, brought to America; Fighting on arrival, fighting for survival.

Words and Music by NOEL WILLIAMS
and BOB MARLEY

COULD YOU BE LOVED

Could you be, could you be, could you be loved, could you be, could you be loved?
Don't let them change you, or even rearrange you, oh no, we've got a life to live.

Words and Music by
BOB MARLEY

GET UP STAND UP

Get up, stand up: stand up for your rights!
Get up, stand up: don't give up the fight!

Words and Music by BOB MARLEY
and PETER TOSH

I SHOT THE SHERIFF

I shot the sheriff, but I didn't shoot no deputy, oh no!
I shot the sheriff, but I swear it was in self-defense.

Words and Music by
BOB MARLEY

IS THIS LOVE

Is this love, is this love, is this love, is this love that I'm feeling?
I, I'm willing and able, so throw my cards on your table.

Words and Music by
BOB MARLEY

JAMMING

Jam's about my pride, and truth I cannot hide to keep you satisfied.
True love that now exists is the love I can't resist, so jam by my side.

Words and Music by
BOB MARLEY

NO WOMAN NO CRY

No woman, no cry; No woman, no cry.
I say, O little darlin', don't shed no tears.
Everything's gonna be alright,
Everything's gonna be alright.

Words and Music by
VINCENT FORD

ONE LOVE

One love. One heart. Let's get together and feel alright.
One love. One heart. Give thanks and praise to the Lord, feel alright.

Words and Music by
BOB MARLEY

REDEMPTION SONG

Emancipate yourselves from mental slavery; won't you help to sing these songs of freedom?
'Cause all I ever had: redemption songs. None but ourselves can free our mind.

Words and Music by
BOB MARLEY

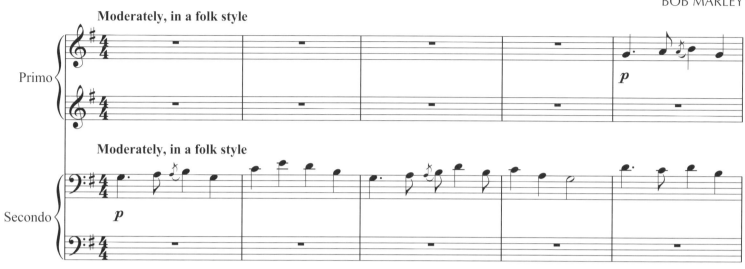

STIR IT UP

Stir it up, little darlin', stir it up, come on, baby.
Come on and stir it up: little darlin', stir it up.

Words and Music by
BOB MARLEY

"One good thing about music, when it hits you, you feel no pain."

Bob Marley (Trench Town Rock)

Bob Marley (1945-1981) is largely regarded as the greatest reggae musician of our time and as a symbol of peace, tolerance, and struggle. Born in a Jamaican village to parents with a 41-year age gap between them, Marley's largely absent white father died when he was 10. His mother, an aspiring Afro-Jamaican singer, then moved with her son to Kingston, seeking a better life. Here, in a squatter settlement known as Trench Town, Marley was exposed to deep poverty and street gangs. But Trench Town was also a vibrant, culturally rich community, and close relationships with like-minded artists and aspiring musicians helped Marley develop his distinctive musical skills and talent.

Though raised Catholic, Marley's interest in the Rastafarian religious and political movements in his late teens profoundly influenced his entire life and music. Many of his songs appear to be relaxed pop tunes about love and loss, but closer study reveals sharp commentary on social justice and equality. Marley survived an assassination attempt but not metastatic melanoma, and died at age 36 in Miami. In 1999 *Time* magazine chose Marley's *Exodus* as their Album of the Century, and the BBC selected "One Love" as the Song of the Millennium. Today his music remains as popular, vital, and timeless as ever.